Shared Governance in Higher Education

AN ATLAS GUIDE

Robert E. Cipriano
and
Jeffrey L. Buller

ATLAS Leadership Publishing
Raleigh, North Carolina

ATLAS Leadership Training
9154 Wooden Road
Raleigh, NC 27617

Book Layout ©2017 BookDesignTemplates.com

Ordering Information:

Quantity sales. Special discounts are available on quantity purchases by corporations, associations, and others. For details, contact the "Special Sales Department" at the address above.

The ATLAS Guide to Shared Governance in Higher Education/ Robert E. Cipriano and Jeffrey L. Buller.—3rd ed.

Contents

The authors would like to thank Sandra McClain for invaluable editorial and research assistance.

If we want to identify the great success of American research universities, and that success goes far beyond Harvard, we have to come back to the question of governance. Excellence requires a firewall between trusteeship, or government ministries, and the academic decision-making process. This American concept of shared governance wherein the faculty are engaged in running the university [is vital] as part of a collaboration with the other stakeholders.

—HENRY ROSOVSKY

CHAPTER 1

An Introduction to Shared Governance

For more than seventy-five years, one of the most important foundations of American higher education has been **shared governance** (Kezar, Lester, and Anderson, 2006, 121). The core idea behind shared governance is that faculty members and administrators both have important roles to play in setting university policy and making key decisions. This principle has received overwhelming support among administrators and faculty alike (Tierney and Minor, 2003, 9). Moreover, many observers believe that active faculty participation in appropriate facets of campus decision-making can improve morale across the institution. For example, the guidelines for the evaluation of administrators established in 2013 by Texas Women's University state the following.

> *Based on the principle of shared governance, regular and formal evaluation of administrators as part of their performance reviews will assist in the development of a greater spirit of collegiality among administrators and faculty, provide more open communication and feedback, promote a more significant role for the faculty in the selection and/or retention of academic administrators, and facilitate greater participation of faculty in the overall administration of the institution within which they play a major role (Administrator Evaluations Task Force, 2013, 2.)*

Nevertheless, while the importance of shared governance has been widely recognized throughout higher education (at least in the United States, Europe, and several other parts of the world), there remains a striking difference of opinion about exactly what *constitutes* shared governance and how it should be practiced within the culture of colleges and universities today. In other words, many people in higher education ask themselves whether the term *shared governance* has become merely a catchphrase that some people use to mean whatever they want it to mean.

A catchphrase is an expression that linguists regard as an *empty* or *floating signifier,* a type of verbal Rorschach inkblot into which people read their own meanings. This idea was first attached to the notion of shared governance in an article by Gary Olson hat appeared in *The Chronicle of Higher Education* back in 2009:

The phrase shared governance is so hackneyed that it is becoming what some linguists call an "empty" or "floating" signifier, a term so devoid of determinate meaning that it takes on whatever significance a particular speaker gives it at the moment. Once a term arrives at that point, it is essentially useless. (Olson, 2009)

But shared governance has the potential of serving a far more important purpose than Olson suggests. As a principle, shared governance is complex. It involves a delicate balance among the responsibilities of the faculty, staff, administration, and governing board when decisions are made and carried out. It involves empowerment and delegation. It requires trust. And as the authors of this guide have learned, it all too frequently results in a great deal of misunderstanding.

Let's begin with one other basic fact noted by Olson in that 2009 article: "**[A]ll legal authority in any university originates from one place and one place only: the governing board**" (Olson, 2009). This basic fact is frequently resisted by the faculty and unknown by the students, and yet it lies at the heart of any true understanding of what shared governance is.

Bob Cipriano, one of the authors of this guide, was once presenting a workshop on academic leadership for faculty members and deans at an American university. A conversation about leadership soon turned to the topic of academic freedom, which subsequently led to a discussion of shared governance. Several questions emerged.

- How is shared governance defined operationally?
- What are the roles and responsibilities of key stakeholders at a college or university?
- Who is invited to "sit at the table" when key decisions are being made?
- How and by whom are policies developed?
- What *should* the governance model be at a college or university?

Many faculty members at Bob's workshop argued vehemently that they are the ones who are recognized experts in their chosen fields and thus they're the ones who have both an obligation and a professional responsibility to make such decisions as:

- whom to hire and whom to terminate among the professoriate
- which of their colleagues they should recommend for tenure, promotion in rank, merit pay increases, and reappointment
- what the content and requirements of the curriculum should be
- which students to accept into their majors

- which courses students must complete in order to graduate

- and other issues related to academic content and staffing.

The deans at the workshop agreed with the faculty to a certain point but they steadfastly disagreed with the faculty on one key issue. Faculty members, the deans stated, merely make *recommendations* to the administration on these issues; it is only the administration (and chiefly the president or chancellor) who is authorized to make *decisions* about these issues.

Who was right in this discussion? The answer to this question could be neither side was right, both of them were, or each side was partly right and partly wrong, depending on how that institution's charter and bylaws are written. As we explain in *The AT-LAS Guide to Leadership in Higher Education*, colleges and universities adhere to a number of different organizational models simultaneously. The type of structure that most people are familiar with in most organizations is a *hierarchy* or *social pyramid*. In this type of structure, power increases as you go up the ranks of the hierarchy, and the number of people increases as you go down the ranks in the hierarchy. (See Figure 1.)

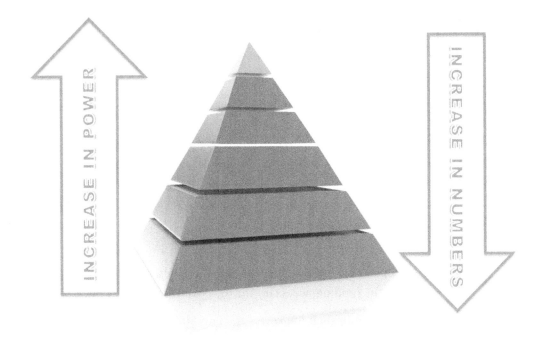

Figure 1. A Hierarchy

An army is a good example of how hierarchies work. The commander-in-chief has a tremendous amount of power, but there's only one such position. There are more generals than there are commanders-in-chief, but generals don't have as much power as the commander-in-chief. There are more colonels than generals, but they have even less power, and so on.

Colleges and universities both do and don't act as this type of hierarchy. For example, on the academic side of the institution, faculty members report to chairs who in turn report to deans who in turn report to the provost (one of the vice presidents) who in turn reports to the president or chancellor. And conversely, the president or chancellor evaluates the provost who in turn evaluates the deans who in turn evaluate the chairs who in turn evaluate the faculty. Moreover, colleges and universities tend to be very strong *social* hierarchies. Whether the result is intentional or not, staff members are often made to feel as thought they're not quite as important as the faculty (at least in the eyes of certain faculty members). Assistant professors are often made to feel as thought they're not quite as important as full professors (at least in the eyes of certain senior faculty members).

But colleges and universities don't always act as hierarchies or social pyramids *when it comes to how decisions are made*. Curricular innovation rarely begins with the president or chancellor; it begins with the faculty, and the approval process moves *up* the pyramid. Promotions in rank don't begin with the president or chancellor; they usually begin with the faculty member who applies for promotion, and the approval process moves *up* the pyramid. Why does "power" in these areas seem to flow in the opposite direction from what we usually see in a hierarchy?

The answer, as we said earlier, is that colleges and universities operate under a number of different organizational models simultaneously. While they function as hierarchies in terms of their organizational charts and their evaluation processes, they often assign power and make decisions according to different organizational structures. One of the most important of these alternative structures is the *distributed organization*, where different kinds of powers are assigned to different branches of the organization. The most familiar example of a distributed organization is the U. S. federal government, which allocates different powers to different branches. (See Figure 2 on page 9.)

- The **legislative branch** creates the laws. It sets policies and appropriates the funding necessary for the government to operate.

- The **judicial branch** interprets the laws. It decides whether legislation accords with the constitution and settles controversies brought before it.

- The **executive branch** implements the laws. It carries out the public policy that has been enacted and funded by the legislative branch and deemed constitutional by the legislative branch.

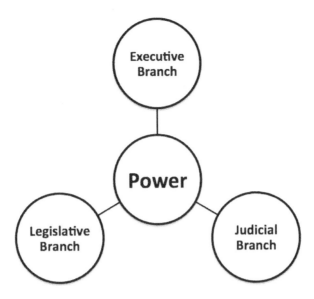

Figure 2. The U. S. Federal Government as a Distributed Organization

In theory these three branches are co-equal. This principle of co-equality means that, instead of a hierarchy, the branches function as a kind of triumvirate with **checks and balances** to insure that any one branch doesn't exceed its authority. We can think of these checks and balances as a kind of **veto power**. Although most people are familiar with the president's ability to veto bills passed by Congress, it's important to recognize that each branch has its own sort of veto power. If the president as commander-in-chief of the armed forces wants to embark on a military enterprise that Congress opposes, Congress can refuse to fund it. This **power of the purse** is thus a form of veto power. If Congress passes a law that the president approves, the legislative branch still has the authority to declare that law unconstitutional, effectively exerting its own type of veto power.

Distributed organizations thus operate through **separation of powers** and, while doing so can slow the process of change and innovation, that result is not accidental. Slowing the process and requiring consensus is a safeguard against embarking on a rash and dangerous action that has not been carefully reviewed. Intentional bottlenecks allow the federal government to try to ascertain what possible consequences may result from a poor decision. This structure was also designed by the framers of the U. S. constitution as a bulwark against tyranny. While the executive branch does have substantial power, it doesn't have *unlimited* power. By design the other two branches are its equals.

There are times when colleges and universities act in a similar way, as their own sort of distributed organizations. The governing board has its unique set of responsibilities.

The administration has its unique set of responsibilities. And the faculty has its unique set of responsibilities. (See Figure 3.)

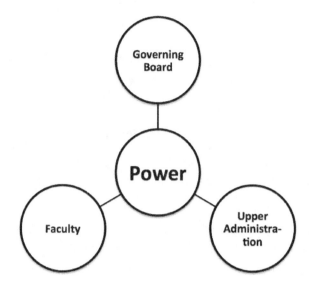

Figure 3. A University as a Distributed Organization

But here's where the difficult part comes in: **Precisely what those responsibilities are depends on the charter and bylaws of the university.** That's why our answer to the question "Who was right, the faculty or the administration, in the debate about decision-making versus recommendations?" had to be "It depends."

- Since the governing board is the one and only place where ultimate legal authority is held, the answer is that, unless authority for promotions and the curriculum have been officially delegated elsewhere, the *governing board* makes the decision, and both the faculty and administration are only making recommendations. In this case, neither the faculty members nor the deans were completely correct in their arguments.

- If the governing board delegated responsibility for curricular and promotion decisions to the administration, then the *administration* decides, and the faculty only recommends. This arrangement is becoming increasingly common (although far from universal) as boards defer to the administration in the areas of curriculum and promotion, retaining for themselves only the right to make sure that existing policies are being adequately followed. In this case, the deans were correct in their argument.

- If the governing board delegated responsibility for curricular and promotion decisions to the faculty (or delegated it to the administration, which in turn delegated it to the faculty), then the *faculty* decides. While uncommon, this arrangement does sometimes occur, particularly at professional schools where the issue of who is legally qualified to teach and what curriculum can be accredited is especially complicated. In this case, the faculty members were correct in their argument.

In order to determine where final authority for these duties has been assigned, it's necessary to review an institution's governance documents. In addition, certain for-profit or privately owned institutions don't fit this model at all. They may even act as hierarchies that are little different from an army or corporation. Nevertheless, the vast majority of colleges and universities in the United States (as well as other countries with similar systems of higher education) do follow certain elements of distributed organizations in their decision-making processes. What is termed *separation of powers* for the U.S. federal government is termed *shared governance in higher education.*

What About Veto Power?

"That may be so," a reader might object, "but you said earlier that distributed organizations grant the different branches veto power. There's no such thing as veto power at a college or university. If the board decides something, the faculty are powerless to veto it." While this sentiment is common, there is in fact a type of veto power for each of the major branches of higher education. If the faculty or administration takes an action that the governing board doesn't approve of, the board can sometimes veto it directly and at other times can block it through the power of the purse. If the faculty takes an action that the administration doesn't approve of, sometimes administrators can veto that action directly and at other times they can block it through the power of the purse. If the governing board takes an action that the administration doesn't approve of, sometimes (like the legislative branch in the U. S. federal government) they can block it through the **power of interpretation**. They can say "how this policy applies to us in terms of day-to-day governance is as follows," even if what then follows isn't at all what the board members originally had in mind. (Compare the difference between the originalists and the progressives on the U. S. Supreme Court.) And if the governing board or the administration takes an action that the faculty doesn't approve of, sometimes it can be blocked through the **power of committees**.

A vast amount of work is done at colleges and universities through committees, councils, task forces, and other working groups. When one of these bodies *slow-walks* an action that the governing board or administration is relying on, the faculty is effectively "vetoing" that action. This strategy is similar to how the filibuster works in the U. S. Congress. By extending a process indefinitely, the faculty at an institution can exert power in a surprisingly large number of areas. A new program that the governing board or administration desperately wants can't be offered until the faculty approves the curriculum and approves the credentials of the instructors. A new administrator that the board or upper administration wants tenured or offered a certain rank often has to be approved by faculty committees. If those committees don't cooperate, the action wanted by the board or upper administration can't occur.

When there is opposition between the faculty and the administration or governing board, faculty members will sometimes say things like, "We can just wait this person out. Students come and go. Board members come and go. Deans come and go. But we're here for the long haul. Time is on our side." As a result, in order for shared governance to work effectively, *each branch of the institution has to be willing to negotiate for what it wants by being willing to compromise on what is within its power to do.*

CHAPTER 2

Challenges to Shared Governance

Perhaps the single most important key to effective shared governance is open and candid communication. When multiple stakeholder groups at an institution are kept informed about current challenges and opportunities, understand what developments are occurring within the institution, and invited to participate in discussions as true partners, the college or university benefits from a broad range of expertise and perspectives. If communication isn't open and candid, unforeseen consequences are more likely to blindside people. Consistent, frank communication means that problems are often identified before they become too severe. And the skills of many highly trained people become available to solve them. For this reason, we might say that shared governance is a type of *academic crowdsourcing*. It gives voice (although not necessarily ultimate *authority*) to all constituencies, helping those who *do* make decisions make them more wisely.

Marietta Del Favero has discussed the way in which administrators and faculty members often have different values, interests, and responsibilities. She notes, for example, that faculty members typically say that they'd like fewer students in their classes as a way of improving pedagogy, while administrators reply that they'd like larger classes as a way of improving productivity. Faculty members prefer to teach students who have scored in the top one percent of standardized admissions tests, while administrators (particularly at tuition-driven institutions) frequently prefer to increase enrollment. (Del Favero, 2003.)

These differences create a challenging but ultimately valuable tension when decisions about higher education need to be made. Faculty members are highly specialized in their particular field of interest. They have a passion for a certain field and spend much of their time completely immersed in that discipline. As a result, they're often not fully aware of broader university goals. They may not see the relationship between occupancy rates in the residence halls, the rising costs of academic journals, or the win-loss record of the football team and the resources they have available for teaching, research, and service. They may regard money spent on administration as a misuse of funding that could be better spent on improving faculty salaries, enhancing classroom facilities, upgrading computers and research equipment, and subventing travel to academic conferences. But they may not understand the high level of accountability and documentation required by legislatures, accrediting bodies, and university systems that today requires a large professional staff simply to track, record, and report all of these institutional data.

As James Duderstadt, the former president of the University of Michigan, puts it,

> *The faculty culture typically holds values that are not necessarily well aligned with those required to manage a complex institution. For example, the faculty values academic freedom and independence, whereas the management of the institution requires responsibility and accountability. Faculty members tend to be individualistic, highly entrepreneurial lone rangers rather than the team players required for management. They tend to resist strong, visionary leadership and firmly defend their personal status quo. It is frequently difficult to get faculty commitment to—or even interest in—broad institutional goals that are not congruent with personal goals. (Tierney, 2004, 144.)*

Conversely, administrators may become overly shortsighted when they favor courses and disciplines that attract large enrollments over those that may help to produce more well-rounded students. They may see the benefits of applied research but fail to recognize how basic research can help to advance society at some distant point in the future. As a result, ongoing conversations among institutional stakeholders are useful in broadening a sort of "tunnel vision" that both faculty members and administrators can develop. Funding is important, administrators come to see, but so is enhancing human understanding. The rich diversity of disciplines that make a university truly universal is crucial, faculty members may conclude, but so is sufficient enrollment to pay the bills.

Because colleges and universities have their own organizational cultures, they require their own approaches to academic leadership. In a traditional hierarchy such as one finds in the military, most corporations, and many athletic teams, leadership largely means directing one's authority downward through the ranks. While *managing up* is increasingly being recognized as an important leadership skill, the vast majority of books written about leadership in hierarchical organizations still focus on the skills associated with *managing down*: decision making, developing and articulating a vision, promoting a sense of authority, being persistent, and gaining the respect of others. Since, as we saw earlier, higher education remains hierarchical to some degree, those skills are still important for academic leaders. But distributed organizations, like the federal government of the United States or most colleges and universities, also demand *other* skills of its leaders. Being able to negotiate, compromise, speak and write effectively, and persuade others with very different worldviews become essential for a leader's long-term success. If a president gets too high-handed with Congress, Congress is likely to thwart the president's initiatives through the power of the purse and its ability to override a veto. And if a university administration gets too high-handed with the faculty, the faculty is likely to thwart the administration's initiatives through the powers that *it* holds: slow-walking proposals through committees, designing curricula that subvert the administration's agenda, and failing to approve the faculty appointments of the people whom the president or chancellor wishes to appoint.

That potential conflict can be complicated even further by the fact that faculty members sometimes have relatively few incentives to participate in institutional governance. Serving on the faculty senate or taking a leadership role in the union typically requires unpaid work in addition to ongoing expectations for progress in teaching, research, and service. Moreover, there is often such a high level of distrust between the faculty and the administration at many institutions that when professors *do* accept formal positions within the administration, they may be viewed by their peers as having "corrupt and venal motives," such as a desire for more money, greater power, and a more luxurious office. Some faculty members even decline administrative positions, although they would have much to offer in those positions, because they feel they'd be "betraying" their colleagues (or because they'd be treated by their colleagues as though they were indeed betraying them).

The result is that administrators are sometimes frustrated by the faculty's reluctance to take advantage of the decision-making opportunities they're given, preferring to become involved only when they object to a specific proposal. (See Association of Governing Boards, 2010, 4 and Birnbaum, 2004, 4-22.) Faculty members who are active in governance at institutions may echo the view that their colleagues do not become sufficiently involved in issues of governance even while they're complaining about administrative encroachments on faculty prerogatives. (See Rhoades, 2005, 38-42.) Whatever the ideal of shared governance should be, it's clear that most colleges and universities still have a long way to go.

CHAPTER 3

Trying to Square the Circle

The frustrations many faculty members feel today is that legislatures, governing boards, and administrations seem increasingly to ignore the distributed culture of the college or university and treat the institution as though it had the hierarchical culture of a corporation. Students are commonly referred to as *customers*, and other terms from the world of business—like *key performance indicators (KPIs)*, *benchmarks*, and *return on investment (ROI)*—are heard despite the fact that professors would prefer to be talking about academic freedom, the community of scholars, critical thinking, research integrity, and the sanctity of tenure.

This effort to "square the circle" of higher education by "making it run more like a business" affects more than just vocabulary. In 1975, state and local governments supported public colleges and universities by providing seventy-five percent of their budgets; by 2019, that figure had decreased to twenty-three percent. This lack of government support has forced public universities to raise tuition and fees dramatically. But there are also other factors contributing to this rise in cost. The budgets of most academic programs devote ninety to ninety-five percent of their resources to personal services (i.e., salaries and benefits). As salaries increase, so do budgetary pressures. Furthermore, costs for technology have risen, and even simple equipment like computers and printers have to be updated regularly. The size of the staff and administration has also increased due to the demands that were mentioned earlier in this guide for more assessment, program review, strategic planning, and other forms of accountability. Student demand has changed, too. Residence halls are now expected to have private rooms and baths at many institutions. Food services offer many more choices than in the past. Recreational facilities have been expanded to keep up with students' expectation.

The result has been a quick and historic rise in costs. In 2008 (the year in which there was a dramatic dip in the stock market), there were only five colleges and universities in the United States that cost fifty thousand dollars or more per year in tuition, room and board. Only one year later that number climbed to fifty-eight colleges and universities. On September 1, 2019, *The New York Times* reported "The *average* annual price tag for attending an American college is now around $50,000." (Zaloom, 2019, SR 4.) Against this backdrop of events, administrators are increasingly expected to raise additional resources for the institution through fundraising and externally supported grants or sponsored research. In fact, many presidents or chancellors say that a majority of their time must now be devoted to raising money and identifying additional donors to their institutions.

The result of these developments is twofold. First, in any discussion of shared governance, it's important to remember that the faculty and the administration are not the only two stakeholders affected by the decisions made at a college or university. When tuition increases, what is the effect on students and/or their parents? When resources are devoted to new classroom buildings, athletic facilities, and residence halls in an effort to attract more and better students, who absorbs those costs if the school's plans to develop additional revenue from tuition aren't successful? Second, in an effort to keep rising costs under control, members of the faculty, staff, and administration are repeatedly asked to do more with less. The increase in workload, decrease in operating budgets, and tightening of standards for tenure and promotion all combine to produce an environment that can lead to burnout. Students are not well served by professors who work more hours with less job satisfaction. The cost of replacing members of the administration and staff who leave their positions because of frustration with their jobs consumes resources that could have been devoted to improving the educational experience for students.

All these challenges indicate why the topic of shared governance remains so important in higher education today. Decisions can't be made by only one stakeholder group since that group has only one perspective. There must be genuine distribution of responsibilities and serious discussions of the impact decisions in admissions, hiring, curriculum, and other key areas have on *all* those in the college or university community. In short, there needs to be a renewed appreciation for what shared governance is and what it can become.

CHAPTER 4

Toward a Renewed Appreciation of Shared Governance

Before anyone can truly appreciate the full value of shared governance, that person must understand what shared governance really means (and, more importantly, what it *doesn't* mean). Bob Cipriano has developed the following quiz that academic leaders can use to launch meaningful conversations with others at their institutions. One way of using the quiz is to have everyone at a meeting or retreat complete it (an answer key follows) and then discuss the issues that it raises.

A Quiz on Shared Governance

PART 1. TRUE OR FALSE. Read each statement and then indicate whether you believe that, on the whole, it is more TRUE than false or more FALSE than true.

Shared governance is:

TRUE	FALSE	1.	a collective lack of responsibility.
TRUE	FALSE	2.	making full use of all the "brainpower" of the institution.
TRUE	FALSE	3.	a synonym for *faculty governance*.
TRUE	FALSE	4.	reflected in a collaborated and collegial environment among the faculty, administration, and governing board.
TRUE	FALSE	5.	administrative autocracy.
TRUE	FALSE	6.	an approach by which authority is clearly assigned and responsibility for results is clearly allocated.
TRUE	FALSE	7.	responsible for gridlock and endless debate.
TRUE	FALSE	8.	addressed in the American Association of University Professor's *Statement on Government of Colleges and Universities*.
TRUE	FALSE	9.	the sole responsibility of the faculty to implement.

TRUE	FALSE	10.	affirmation that institutional decision-making should be conducted jointly by the board, administration, and faculty and that the faculty should have primary responsibility for decisions about the curriculum, academic policy, and faculty personnel matters.
TRUE	FALSE	11.	the sole responsibility of the administration.
TRUE	FALSE	12.	a shared understanding that faculty representatives and administrators should strive for informed mutual support.

PART 2. MULTIPLE CHOICE. Read each statement and then circle the *one response* that is closest to how you feel about the statement.

1. Shared governance at colleges and universities is a principle that is fundamental for the inclusion of the perspectives of key stakeholder groups in major areas of institutional responsibility and decision-making.
    a. Yes. I firmly believe this.
    b. I believe this but something else is missing.
    c. I would need more information before I could say whether I believed this or not.
    d. This statement is far too vague. What does it really mean?
    e. That's an attractive ideal, but the real world doesn't work that way.
    f. No. I don't believe this.

2. Shared Governance should be viewed as a set of guidelines about the roles, responsibilities, and authority of the governing board, faculty, and administration in such matters as curricular decisions, the allocation of the budget, and other important areas involving how the institution functions.
    a. Yes. I firmly believe this.
    b. I believe this but something else is missing.
    c. I would need more information before I could say whether I believed this or not.
    d. This statement is far too vague. What does it really mean?
    e. That's an attractive ideal, but the real world doesn't work that way.
    f. No. I don't believe this.

Once people at the meeting or retreat have completed this quiz, you can launch a discussion of shared governance in the following way. You can note that, for Part 1, there are some answers that are right and some answers that are wrong. And for those items that are less clear cut, there is at least a broad consensus throughout higher education. And the quiz is very easy to "grade": Even-numbered statements are true; odd-numbered statements are false. Part 2, on the other hand, merely reflects how each person who took the quiz *feels* about shared governance. Areas of strong agreement or disagreement then provide good material with which to begin a fruitful discussion.

In order to make the resulting discussion as fruitful as possible, you may want to consider adding some additional information. Struck by how diverse the perception of shared governance was among full-time faculty members, Bob Cipriano and his research associate Richard L. Riccardi surveyed all full-time faculty members working at four universities in the northeastern United States. A total of 1,100 surveys were distributed, with 232 surveys completed, yielding a response rate of 21.1%. The three-part, four-page questionnaire that Cipriano and Riccardi used had several parts. Part I included 37 true/false questions dealing with the respondent's perceptions of shared governance. Each time a respondent regarded a statement as true, he or she was asked to indicate the level of importance he or she attached to that statement.

Part Two of the survey asked respondents to indicate and rank what they considered to be the five most important aspects of shared governance. Part Three consisted of eight questions regarding the demographics of the people responding to the survey, such as their gender, rank, highest degree held, and years of service in higher education. The demographic questions were added to determine whether any patterns emerged in the data, such as men answering one way and women another or full professors responding differently from assistant professors.

More than 90% of the respondents indicated that 24 of the 37 statements in Part I were true. These statements concerned a variety of issues, ranging from principles of communication to academic freedom to collegiality. The top five statements about the principles of shared governance that respondents listed as true were:

1. A high quality of education and scholarship is strengthened where there is a genuine culture of shared governance. (99.1%)

2. Shared governance activities may involve discussion. (98.7%)

3. Shared governance activities may involve collaboration. (98.3%)

4. The principles of shared governance emanate from the belief that faculty members are in the best position to shape and implement curriculum. (98.3%)

5. Shared governance activities may involve decision-making. (97.8%)

When the respondents were then asked to rank the same 37 statements according to their importance (with 1 being the least important and 4 being the most important), the following five statements rose to the top of the list:

1. The principles of shared governance emanate from the belief that faculty members are in the best position to shape and implement the curriculum. (3.67)

2. Faculty participation in shared governance is essential to the well-being of the university. (3.58)

3. The principles of shared governance emanate from the belief that faculty members are in the best position to select their academic colleagues. (3.53)

4. Faculty participation in shared governance is essential to promote and encourage a diversity of ideas. (3.49)

5. Shared governance activities may involve decision-making. (3.49)

In Part Two of the survey, the researchers were offered a glimpse into how faculty members as a group tended to view shared governance. Participants were asked to list in an open-ended format what they regarded as the most important aspects of shared governance. Typical responses included:

- An opportunity for all stakeholders to participate in important decision-making processes

- Protection from an administration that has become too powerful

- A collective voice that represents a significant diversity of views

- Democratic participation in university life and culture

- A clear faculty voice in such matters as curriculum, hiring, and academic policy

- Efforts to promote and maintain academic excellence, particularly in the areas of scholarship and teaching

- Creating a climate in which participation and engagement are valued

Cipriano and Riccardi found it interesting that positive terms like *climate*, *culture*, and *curriculum* often stood side by side with what they regarded as more negative or critical sentiments, such as:

- The higher your role in the administration, the more you should serve rather than rule.

- Shared governance helps to keep administrative arrogance in check.

- Shared governance brings an end to secrecy and special deals.

- Shared governance gives a voice to the weak.

- Shared governance means no retaliation.

- Shared governance keeps the university's focus on expanding knowledge, not on job training.

- Shared governance means that the judgment of scholarship remains in the hands of scholars.

- Shared governance implies recognition that without the faculty, the students would not be here.

- Shared governance is a myth; the only thing left in the control of faculty is the curriculum.

- Shared governance means using the faculty to balance the incompetence of administration (and vice versa).

In the next phase of their analysis, Cipriano and Riccardi used textual analysis to categorize the responses they received in terms of general areas of concern. A response received five points if the respondent assigned it the highest level of importance, four points for the second level of importance, three points for the third level, and so on. Using this method, the researchers then ranked the issues raised by faculty members by how important most respondents regarded them. In priority order, the key issues were as outlined in Figure 4 on the next page.

Among these fifteen areas of governance seen in Figure 4, two were clearly regarded by the faculty as most important—**collegiality** and **collaboration**—with **academic excellence** and **decision-making** not far behind. Three additional areas of concern were also regarded as significant—**academic freedom**, **culture**, and **communication**—with the remaining issues assigned far less importance.

Areas of concern	#1	#2	#3	#4	#5	Total Score
1. Collegiality	19	26	14	10	10	271
2. Collaboration	26	19	15	7	5	270
3. Academic Excellence	19	12	20	16	10	245
4. Decision Making	14	21	16	9	9	229
5. Academic Freedom	21	9	12	12	10	211
6. Culture	9	11	14	26	28	211
7. Communication	18	13	13	10	3	204
8. Accountability	11	14	12	9	5	170
9. Curriculum	17	11	5	3	2	152
10. Personnel Matters	4	9	15	15	9	140
11. Inclusion	5	6	10	11	6	107
12. Promotion and Tenure	8	10	2	1	4	92
13. Responsibility	3	12	1	6	8	86
14. Democracy	4	4	10	5	6	82
15. Consensus Building	3	1	5	5	7	51

Figure 4. Textual Analysis by Cipriano and Riccardi

The researchers also wanted to determine who or what specific positions, offices, or centers faculty members tended to regard as the primary *instruments* of shared governance at their institutions. "Which of the following," the respondents were asked, "play a major role in promoting shared governance?" Respondents could specify as many people or groups as they felt were appropriate.

- 82.8% named the president as playing a major role in promoting shared governance.

- 79.3% named the provost.

- 78.4% named the faculty senate or its equivalent.

- 76.3% named the full-time faculty.

- 73.7% named the American Association of University Professors (AAUP) . [NOTE: Each of the four campuses is unionized, and the AAUP plays a dominant role on these campuses.]

- 66.8% named the department chairs.

- 58.6% named "all employees of the university."

Cipriano and Riccardi then asked department chairs the same questions that were posed the faculty. The goal was to determine whether there was any significant difference between how department chairs and faculty members viewed share governance. A total of 114 surveys were distributed of which 35 were returned: a response rate of 30.7%. The data was then processed in the same way it was for faculty members. Figure 5 on the next page summarizes how the chairs ranked various areas of concern in order of importance.

As expected by the researchers, both department chairs and faculty members included *academic excellence* and *academic freedom* among their top five concerns. Among the professoriate (and other studies conducted by the same researchers indicated that department chairs almost always see themselves as part of the professoriate rather than primarily as administrators) academic excellence and academic freedom were regarded as of fundamental importance in higher education. What is more surprising, however, is that *decision making* also ranked high on both lists, illustrating the desire among the professoriate for college professors to be "seated at the table" when major decisions are being made.

Similarities and differences among how faculty members and department chairs viewed various areas of concern relevant in discussions of shared governance can best be seen by comparing their results side by side as can be seen in Figure 6 on page 26.

Area of Concern	Average Importance	#1	#2	#3	#4	#5	Score
Academic Excellence	3.79	14	3	2	1		90
Academic Freedom	3.82	3	9	3	3	2	68
Communication	3.80	3	5	3	1	3	49
Decision Making	3.59	2	4	2	6	1	45
Promotion & Tenure	3.74	1	2	8	3	2	45
Curriculum	3.51	2	6	1	2		41
Collaboration	3.56	5		2	2	2	37
Accountability	3.71			6	3	7	31
Responsibility	3.62	1	1	2	7	20	
Collegiality	3.46	1	2		3	3	19
Culture	3.15	2		1			13
Consensus Building	3.45			2	3		12
Inclusion	3.36		1	1		3	10
Personnel Matters	3.24	1			4		9
Democracy	3.29		1		1	1	7

Figure 5. Areas of Concern as Ranked by Department Chairs

Rank	Chairs	Faculty
1	Academic Excellence	Collegiality
2	Academic Freedom	Collaboration
3	Communication	Academic Excellence
4	Decision Making	Decision Making
5	Promotion & Tenure	Academic Freedom

Figure 6. Comparison of Results: Chairs and Faculty

Also, in contrast to how faculty members responded to the survey, department chairs tended to identify the faculty senate as having a greater role in shared governance while they assigned the AAUP and the rest of the university less of a significant role. This difference may have occurred because department chairs are more involved than most faculty members in the governance process of the university and thus have a different view of the role that various stakeholder groups *actually* play in making decisions. We can see this difference of perspective more clearly in Figure 7 on the next page.

Who Plays a Significant Role in Shared Governance?	Chairs	Faculty
President	88.6%	82.8%
Provost	80.0%	79.3%
Faculty Senate	94.3%	78.4%
Full-Time Faculty	74.3%	76.3%
AAUP	54.3%	73.7%
Department Chairs	74.3%	66.8%
All Employees of the University	40.0%	58.6%

Figure 7. Who Plays a Significant Role in Shared Governance?

Cipriano and Riccardi found it interesting to note that faculty members ranked the office of the president as the primary locus of shared governance on campus (82%), while chairs indicated the president was only the *second* most important person for promoting shared governance (88.6%) with primary importance reserved for the faculty senate. Both faculty members and the department chairs did, however, list the president, the provost, and the faculty senate as among the top three offices in terms of promoting shared governance across the institution.

NOTE: The material in this section was adapted from Cipriano and Riccardi, 2009, 4-5.

CHAPTER 5

What Colleges and Universities Say About Shared Governance

Another way of promoting productive conversations about shared governance at your institution is to provide people with information about what *other* colleges and universities say about this topic and then ask people whether they agree with the perspectives of their colleagues elsewhere. For example, in 2005, the University of Arizona noted the following:

> *The success of the University and the positive morale of the faculty and administration are dependent upon continued use of the collective intelligence of the university community. ... This requires extensive sharing of information and a shared understanding that faculty representatives and administrations strive always for informed mutual support through shared governance dialogue. (Fish, 2007, 9-13.)*

Note the following assumptions present in this statement.

- The success of the university in maintaining the positive morale of faculty and administration is highly reliant, if not totally dependent, on continued use of the **collective intelligence** of the university.

- Shared governance requires **extensive sharing of information** and a **shared understanding** that faculty representatives and administrators strive always for **informed mutual support** through shared governance **dialogue.**

In a similar way, a statement on shared governance that appears on a website page dealing with unionization at the University of Washington underscores that institution's strong commitment to the inclusion of faculty in discussions about important decisions.

> *Since as early as 1956 with the adoption of our General Policy in Section 13-20 of the Faculty Code, we have been committed to a joint faculty-administration relationship that manages our complex interests and common objectives. We believe shared gov-*

ernance between the faculty and the administration is the best way to advance our mission and status as a world-class university. We are proud of our track record of collaboration at all levels of operation–institutional, school/college/campus, and department/program.

We want to be clear on this point: our faculty members play a critical role in the management of the university. This collaborative decision-making is seen frequently in the Faculty Senate, which serves as the legislative and executive agency of the Faculty, but it goes much further. Our system of joint leadership also includes a wide-ranging matrix of advisory and decision-making bodies that include college councils, executive committees, search committees, promotion and tenure committees and more. (Shared Governance at the UW, 2019.)

The University of Washington's statement continues that the institution's faculty councils and committees, faculty groups at the level of school, college, or campus, and the secretary of the faculty (an elected officer of the faculty who advises the administration on faculty rights and responsibilities) all join the faculty senate in playing an important role in promoting shared governance at the institution.

The University of Louisiana at Monroe (ULM) defines shared governance as

the process by which the University community (i.e., faculty, staff, administrators, alumni, and students) has the opportunity to influence decisions on matters of policy and procedure, and/or an opportunity to present alternatives on such matters. The objective of shared governance is to foster mutually reinforcing relationships that expand the opportunities for cooperation and leadership while facilitating judicious, yet creative, university governance.

Shared Governance includes issues of values, culture, management, and administration, as well as operating frameworks, such as legislation, which are externally imposed. The intent of this process is to balance efficiency and effectiveness with equity and fairness. (Shared Governance: The University of Louisiana at Monroe, 2019.)

ULM has also developed an extensive guide titled *Principles and Practices of Shared Governance* (2007) that covers such topics as appropriate representation, procedural integrity, and what shared governance means in actual practice at the institution. A useful discussion can be held by distributing copies of the ULM guide and then asking the following questions: "If our own institution were to draft a similar document about shared governance, what similar sections would be included? What might we omit from the ULM guide? What should be added?"

At the University of Baltimore (UB) the concept of shared governance is expanded to include the perspectives of staff members and students.

> *Shared governance gives opportunities to faculty, staff, students and administrators to participate, appropriate to their special knowledge and expertise, in decisions affecting the institution. All constituencies are encouraged to be active participants in their representative UB council or senate. (Shared Governance: The University of Baltimore, 2019.)*

The committees described at UB as playing a significant role in shared governance are the student government association, the faculty senate, the staff senate, and the governance steering council. The institution's website notes that "The University of Baltimore is committed to engaging adjunct faculty members and graduate assistants in campus dialogue to inform decisions affecting the institution." (Shared Governance: The University of Baltimore, 2019.)

The definition of shared governance at the State University of New York (SUNY) is similarly broad.

> *"Shared governance" in higher education refers to structures and processes through which faculty, professional staff, administration, governing boards and, sometimes, students and staff participate in the development of policies and in decision-making that affect the institution. (Campus Governance Leaders Toolkit, 2019.)*

Nevertheless, the SUNY system's definition also adds one critical distinction.

> *While the administration and governing board of the institution are compelled to consider the campus governance body's resolutions and recommendations, they are not required to accept or implement them. (Campus Governance Leaders Toolkit, 2019.)*

The University of California (UC) regards shared governance as a balance between opportunity and responsibility. A statement prepared by the UC faculty senate notes that shared governance

> *imposes on faculty a measure of responsibility for the manner in which the University operates. Faculty participation in governance of the University through the agency of the Academic Senate is a guiding force that unifies the ten campuses of the University into a single system under a uniform standard of excellence. (Simmons, 2009.)*

At UC by standing order of the Board of Regents and other institutional policies, the faculty senate is authorized to determine the conditions for admission, certificates, and degrees (other than honorary degrees), authorize and supervise all courses and curricula, determine the membership of faculties, and engage in similar activities on behalf of the university.

In addition to these institutional policies, the American Association of University Professors (AAUP) has developed a policy on shared governance that can provide the basis for a fruitful campus conversation. The AAUP's Committee of College and University Governance composed its first statement on shared governance in 1920, emphasizing the importance of faculty involvement in personnel decisions, selection of administrators, preparation of budgets, and determination of educational policies. Refinements were added when the AAUP's 1966 *Statement on Governance of Colleges and Universities* was published.

Key statements made by the AAUP on the issue of shared governance include the following.

Understanding, based on community of interest and producing joint effort, is essential for at least three reasons. First, the academic institution, public or private, often has become less autonomous: buildings, research, and student tuition are supported by funds over which the college or university exercises a diminishing control. Legislative and executive authorities, at all levels, play a part in the making of important decisions in academic policy. If these voices and forces are to be successfully heard and integrated, the academic institution must be in a position to meet them with its own generally unified view. Second, regard for the welfare of the institution remains important despite the mobility and interchange of scholars. Third, a college or university in which all the components of their interdependence, of the usefulness of communication among themselves, and of the force of joint action will enjoy increased capacity to solve educational problems.

The variety and complexity of the tasks performed by institutions of higher education produce an inescapable interdependency among governing board, administration, faculty, students, and others. The relationship calls for adequate communication among those components, and full opportunity for appropriate joint planning efforts.

When an educational goal has been established, it becomes the responsibility of the faculty to determine the appropriate curriculum and procedures of student instruction.

Such matters as major changes in the size or composition of the student body and the relative emphasis to be given to the various elements of the educational and research program should involve participation of governing board, administration, and faculty prior to final decision.

The Faculty:

The faculty has primary responsibility for such fundamental areas as curriculum, subject matter and methods of instruction, research, faculty status, and those aspects of student life that relate to the educational process. On these matters the power of review or final decision lodged in the governing board or delegated by it to the president should be exercised only in exceptional circumstances, and for reasons communicated to the faculty. It is desirable that the faculty should, following such communi-

cation, have opportunity for further consideration and further transmittal of its views to the president or board. Budgets, personnel limitations, the time element, and the policies of the groups, bodies, and agencies having jurisdiction may set limits to realization of faculty advice.

The faculty sets the requirements for the degrees offered in course, determines when the requirements have been met, and authorizes the president and board to grant the degrees thus achieved.

Faculty status and related matters are primarily a faculty responsibility; this area includes appointments, reappointments, decisions not to reappoint, promotions, the granting of tenure, and dismissal. The primary responsibility of the faculty for such matters is based upon the fact that its judgment is central to general educational policy. Furthermore, scholars in a particular field or activity have the chief competence for judging the work of their colleagues; in such competency it is implicit that responsibility exists for both adverse and favorable judgments. Likewise, there is the more general competence of experienced faculty personnel committees having a broader charge. Determination in these matters should first be by faculty action through established procedures, reviewed by the chief academic officers with the concurrence of the board. The governing board and president should, on questions of faculty status, as in other matters where the faculty has primary responsibility, concur with the faculty judgment except in rare instances and for compelling reasons, which should be stated in detail. (Text adapted from Statement on Government of Colleges and Universities, n.d.)

The AAUP's statement suggests that the board, administration, and faculty should conduct institutional decision-making *jointly* and that the faculty should have "primary responsibility" for decisions about the curriculum, academic policy, and faculty personnel matters. It recommends that the governing board and upper administration respect the faculty's role in shaping the curriculum with regard to which courses will be offered, what the requirements will be for graduation, how courses will be sequenced, what the content of those courses should be, and similar matters. The idea behind these recommendations is that academic policies should fall within the purview of the faculty because those who serve on the faculty have a greater depth of academic knowledge in their specialties than administrators can have. For this reason, a high level of instruction and scholarship can only occur in a culture of genuine shared governance.

What Is A Healthy Shared Governance Model?

In light of these policies and the history of higher education, the authors of this guide would like to propose that a healthy shared governance model has the following characteristics.

1. There should be clear delineation of which constituency groups at the institution have final decision-making authority over which area, which groups must be consulted, and which groups must be informed.

2. There should be a commitment to erring on the side of too much discussion and consultation rather than too little.

3. Guidelines should be established for how decisions by various constituencies are to be made and how dissent from those decisions is to be expressed.

This model will, of course, be implemented differently at public universities and private universities, large schools with multi-layered hierarchies, and small schools with relatively flat administrative structures. But it is in the interest of students, the community, other stakeholders in higher education, and the independence of research that these three characteristics be discussed at every college and university in an effort to make higher education sustainable and increasingly relevant for the future.

CHAPTER 6

Higher Education Is Changing

The world of academia is changing so rapidly that it's difficult (some might even say impossible) to keep up with what is different today from the way things were ten years ago or one year ago or perhaps last week. But when the authors visit various campuses, one question that's increasingly asked is, "To whom does the university really belong?"

There are many stakeholders in higher education today, including:

- students
- alumni
- donors
- faculty members
- staff members

- voters
- legislators
- members of the governing board
- presidents, chancellors, CEOs
- other administrators

The authors of this guide believe that, in the changing world of higher education today, colleges and universities need more shared governance, not less. Each of the stakeholder groups listed above brings a different perspective and valuable insights to the discussion of what the college or university of the future must become. Many issues in higher education must still be decided.

- To what extent should an institution's mission be devoted to professional training versus providing a liberal education? How can the goal of providing the employees of the future be balanced with the goal of providing the citizens of the future?

- How can the desire of many students for educational opportunities that are provided 24/7 and in the precise areas they want best be accommodated? *Should* it be accommodated?

- How does an institution balance the need for productivity and sustainability with the pedagogical goal of providing each student with individual attention and support?

- What is the best mix of introductory, intermediate, and advanced courses for the type of students who enroll at each institution?

- How should scarce resources be allocated? Do the facilities that tend to attract students to an institution best serve their needs once they're enrolled?

- What is the proper balance between teaching and research for faculty members at a college or university? How does service fit into this mix?

- What is the best way of addressing the needs of students who require remediation before participating in post-secondary education?

- How should tuition rates be set to accommodate students with low incomes while still covering the institution's expenses?

- Which group of students does each institution serve? Citizens or foreign students? Those who live locally or those who might live anywhere?

At the root of all these questions is a larger question: What is the purpose of a college or university today? That is a question that no single stakeholder group can answer on its own. And that is yet another reason why the principle of shared governance remains consistently important in the rapidly changing landscape of higher education.

CHAPTER 7

Final Observations

While conducting workshops dealing with shared governance on college campuses, the authors of this guide have found that three principles are consistently regarded as of primary importance by both faculty members and department chairs: **Academic Excellence, Collegiality,** and **Decision-Making.** In addition, the importance of shared governance structures such as a faculty senate or university council cannot be overestimated because it is in these bodies that candid discussions may be held about decisions that have a direct impact on the professoriate and on academic issues. In order to create an atmosphere where shared governance is possible, support must come from the top of the institutional hierarchy while also being protected vigilantly by the faculty as a means of promoting inclusive decision-making, collegiality throughout the institution, and progress toward the goal of academic excellence.

Although the American Association of University Professor's *Statement on Government of Colleges and Universities* recognized that final institutional authority resides ultimately in the governing board and that boards regularly entrust the day-to-day administration of the university to the chief executive officer, that statement does not conceive of the college or university in starkly hierarchical terms. To the contrary, it portrays the well-run university as one in which the board and president delegate decision-making power in academic matters to the faculty. This delegation of responsibility to the professoriate is founded on the assumption that faculty members are not merely employees in the traditional sense, but rather are highly trained professionals whose education, knowledge, and experience grants them certain responsibilities. In other words, faculty members are uniquely qualified to exercise decision-making authority in their areas of expertise. Because the faculty's professional judgment needs to be respected in academic matters, professors should be regarded as being in the best position to judge the quality of their colleagues' work, whether time-limited faculty contracts should be renewed, who is deserving of promotion in rank, who should be granted tenure, and other decisions related to their central responsibilities of teaching, research, and service. In the words of one of the twentieth century's greatest university presidents, Robert Maynard Hutchins (1899-1977) of the University of Chicago,

"We get the best results in education and research if we leave their management to people who know something about them." (Hutchins, 1936, 21).

In sum, shared governance is an ideal that is never perfectly attained but that all colleges and universities must continue to strive for. Administrators speak of the importance of shared governance almost as often as do faculty members. But the expression *shared governance* all too frequently means different things to different people. Using this guide as a springboard for an institution-wide conversation about what shared governance really is can be an important first step toward making sure that this key requirement for robust higher education continues to thrive. Ongoing conversations involving administration and faculty can help clarify how shared governance can best be pursued at your specific institution. These conversations are becoming particularly important as increasing numbers of so-called "contingent faculty members," such as adjuncts and those on a term-limited contract, are providing instruction at colleges and universities of all kinds. In addition, there are remote faculty members who may never set foot on the college's campus because they work exclusively online, and their role in the institution's governance needs to be considered in order for all important voices to be heard. For all these reasons, therefore, faculty members and administrators should reflect on how shared governance helps to promote the teaching, research, and service missions of higher education and how this cornerstone of intellectual life can best be preserved.

CHAPTER 8

Questions for Reflection

Questions for Reflection

1. What has been your own experience with shared governance? Is the expression *shared governance* merely a catchphrase with dramatically different meanings for different people?

2. At your own institution, how do you believe most faculty members define the expression *shared governance*? How would the upper administration define it? How would the governing board define it?

3. At your own institution, are there clearly defined roles and responsibilities for the faculty, staff, administration, and governing board? Are those roles and responsibilities accurately followed, or do some groups overstep their bounds?

4. Do you believe that the concept of shared governance has outlived its usefulness? Is shared governance as important now as it was near the start of the twentieth century?

5. If your institution were to draft a statement on shared governance, would it be as inclusive as the statement developed by the University of Baltimore presented in this guide?

6. The Faculty Personnel Office at the University of Louisville has posted online an informative document titled *Shared Governance: It's Happening Here*. You can find this document at http://louisville.edu/provost/what-we-do/SharedGovernance.pdf. Download the document, read it, and then reflect on the following:

   - Do you agree with how the University of Louisville defines *shared governance*? Does their definition go far enough? Too far?

   - What *institutional committees and councils* at the University of Louisville seem to hold primary responsibility for shared governance? What are the equivalents of these committees and councils at your institution?

- What *individuals* at the University of Louisville seem to hold primary responsibility for shared governance? What are the equivalents of these individuals at your institution?

- What does the University of Louisville say about good faith and the principle of dissent? Would such a statement be possible at your own institution?

CHAPTER 9

Key Points in This Guide

○ While the expression *shared governance* is commonly used in higher education, there is surprisingly little agreement about what this term means. In particular, faculty members and administrators tend to view shared governance quite differently.

○ Colleges and universities both do and don't act as hierarchies. On the academic side of the institution, faculty members report to chairs who in turn report to deans who in turn report to the provost (one of the vice presidents) who in turn reports to the president or chancellor. But colleges and universities sometimes don't act as hierarchies or social pyramids when it comes to how decisions, particularly academic decisions, are made.

○ Perhaps the most important key to effective shared governance is open and candid communication.

○ Administrators are often frustrated by the faculty's reluctance to take advantage of the decision-making opportunities they're given, preferring to become involved only when they object to a specific proposal.

○ In a survey conducted by Robert E. Cipriano and Richard L. Riccardi, the researchers discovered that the issues regarded as of prime importance by faculty members are (in order of significance) collegiality, collaboration, academic excellence, decision-making, academic freedom, culture, and communication.

○ When the same survey was presented to department chairs, the issues regarded as of prime importance were (again in order of significance) academic excellence, academic freedom, communication, decision making, and promotion and tenure.

○ The ability of faculty members to "see the world" as administrators see it (and vice versa) is a valuable prerequisite to constructive institution-wide discussions of shared governance.

Many excellent policies on shared governance exist at colleges and universities. If your institution is seeking to create such a statement, it is not necessary to start from scratch. A survey of existing policies is an excellent place to begin..

CHAPTER 10

Six Case Studies for Further Practice

Although the topic of shared governance raises many theoretical concerns, it's difficult to appreciate the full importance of this topic until you have to make actual decisions within a shared governance framework. In other words, you can't really *understand* shared governance until you've *practiced* it for a while.

We can't provide you with actual immersion in shared governance, but we'd like to do the next best thing. In this chapter, you'll find six hypothetical case studies that will require you to approach issues of shared governance from several different perspectives. Although later in this guide you'll find our suggestions about how best to handle the issues in each case, don't immediately proceed to that section after reading the scenarios. Instead, formulate your own ideas about how best to proceed and then compare your ideas to the suggestions we provide.

Case Study #1: Who's Responsible for Class Size?

Imagine that you're a tenured full professor who has chaired a small but highly successful department for the past ten years. You've formed a close-knit group with the three other full-time faculty members in your unit and have a record of making decisions in a collegial, consensus-based manner. Members of your program have become so close, in fact, that it's become a tradition for all four of you to have lunch together every Friday. You look forward to these social gatherings as a way of relieving the pressures of work. Discussions over lunch rarely focus on the work-related issues or your professional lives. Instead, you spend your time talking about your families, children and grandchildren, travel plans, and hobbies.

Despite there being only four of you on the faculty, your department is commonly described as "bursting at the seams" when it comes to students. This year, for example, your program has more than six hundred undergraduate majors. For this reason, as chair you've reluctantly had to devote more and more of your budget to hiring adjuncts and professional advisors as a way of handling this massive student load. You've cut expenditures where you could, but each year you have to cut deeper and deeper. Over time, allocations for conference travel, equipment upgrades, subscriptions to professional journals, and even photocopying class handouts have all been reduced to the bare minimum. Your institution is highly tuition driven, and all departments are under constant pressure from the president, provost, and dean to raise enrollment caps and to recruit and retain more students as a way of making the budget more sustainable.

One evening you receive an email message from your supervisor, Dean Dina Deane, bearing the subject line "**URGENT!!!!!** My Office at **10:30 am** TOMORROW!!!" In her message, Dean Deane tells you to clear your schedule because she has a critical matter to discuss with you, although she doesn't tell you what that matter actually is.

After spending a restless evening thinking of several possibilities (along with their unpleasant consequences) for your discussion, you arrive at Dean Deane's office the following morning. Without any preliminaries, she simply hands you a memo and instructs you to read it. The document is brief and filled, like her email message, with capitalizations, exclamation points, and bold-faced type. In a few lines, the memo informs you that your program has not met its assigned enrollment target for the year and that you are, therefore, to develop a new plan, which the dean must approve, that will recruit additional students into your major and improve retention. The new target you are given is to recruit an additional 75 new majors next year, 85 the following year, and ten more each year for the next five years. In addition, you are to improve your retention rate by no fewer than five percent a year until it rises from its current level of 78% to be no less than 92% in three years.

You're shocked by this demand—of all the unpleasant things you imagined would happen at this meeting, increasing an already unwieldy student-to-teacher ratio wasn't one of them—and you begin to outline reasons why the dean's request will be impossible to meet. Emotionlessly Dean Deane responds that her memo is not a request; it's a requirement. "There's nothing here to negotiate." She indicates that your department must stop acting as though it weren't part of the college. "I need you all to be team players," she says. "It's time for you and everyone else in the department to step up and do your part for the good of this institution."

You ask Dean Deane if other departments have similarly been instructed to recruit significant more students into their majors and to meet such an ambitious retention goal. She becomes angry and refuses to answer the question. "Just let *me* worry about what goes on in other departments! You take care of your own program; I'll take care of the college, thank you very much. You can go now. You have your instructions. I expect you to follow them."

You immediately return to your department and call a special meeting of your colleagues. You show the memo to the other members of the department and reiterate what the dean told you. The other faculty members are incensed. The spirit in the room verges on open rebellion. After a heated discussion, your three colleagues storm out of the room, only to return fifteen minutes later with a letter that all three have signed. It's a formal proposal to establish an entry requirement for students wishing to major in your program. From now on, the letter states, no student will be accepted into your major unless that student has a cumulative grade point average of 3.50 or higher, has successfully completed an advanced course in statistics with a minimum level of B, and has been certified by the Department of Foreign Languages and Literatures as having attained fluency in at least one language other than English. In addition, any student who receives a grade lower than A- in any course offered by your program will immediately be dropped from the major. The letter outlines several reasons why changes in the job market and requirements for admission to graduate and professional programs have made these new standards necessary.

You look around the room and can barely recognize the three colleagues with whom you share lunch each Friday. They look at you as though you're no longer one of them but now merely a mouthpiece for the administration. Even without reviewing individual student records, you estimate that no more than five to ten percent of your current majors would meet the requirements your colleagues have outlined in their letter. As a result, rather than improving your program's recruitment and retention of students, what your colleagues want to do will reduce your number of student majors to a small fraction of what it is now.

You know the other members of your program well enough to realize that, even though they've justified their actions, what they're suggesting cannot be a serious proposal. They are obviously responding out of anger, believing that they have not been treated fairly.

You respond by telling your colleagues that they can't actually do what they propose. They counter by saying, "We just did. Programs have the right to set their own admission standards and requirements for adequate progress in the program. We're merely exercising the authority that's been given us. If you refuse to sign this letter, the vote will still be three to one. Even so, we'd rather not override you on this issue. We've always been a collegial group in the past. So, the question is: Are you with us or against us? After all, we have the principle of shared governance on our side."

1. If you *had* to choose one of the following responses, which of these would you choose? Why?

a. I would ask Dean Deane to meet with the faculty of the department to discuss the contents of her memo as well as the department's response.

b. I would resign as chair.

c. I would sign the faculty's document, forming a united front with my colleagues.

d. I would earnestly begin to recruit more undergraduate students into my department and to improve our retention rate.

e. I would ask other chairs what they would do if they were in my situation.

f. I would file a grievance against Dean Deane for her treatment of me and my program.

g. I would reach out to my statewide professional organization for support.

h. I would reach out to my national professional organization for support.

i. I would research the topic of shared governance to see if any established precedent on this issue can help my case.

j. I would bring the matter up at a meeting of the Faculty Senate.

k. I would speak to the provost about Dean Deane's mandate.

l. I would organize the students in my department to protest the dean's action.

m. I would organize the parents of our program's current majors to write letters to the dean, denouncing her action.

n. I would organize alumni to denounce the dean's decision.

o. I would start looking for another job at another institution.

2. If your options were *not* limited to those listed under #1, what would you do?

Case Study # 2: Different Perspectives on Shared Governance

You are a tenured associate professor at a university where full-time faculty members traditionally teach three courses per semester. Your associate dean, Dr. Terry Fied, asks you to serve on the search committee for a new dean of your college. Doing so will be a time-consuming task: There will be meetings every Friday afternoon; you will have to review well more than a hundred applications, check each candidate's references, and be available nearly all day whenever a finalist is brought to campus. Nevertheless, you have strong opinions about the sort of leadership your college needs. So, you tell Dr. Fied that you'll serve on the search committee but only if your teaching load can be reduced to two courses a semester until the search is completed.

Dr. Fied responds, "I can't do that. And I'm surprised that you'd ask. You know better than anyone how short-staffed we are. If I reduce your load, everyone on the committee will want me to do the same thing for them, and we won't be able to offer enough classes to meet student demand."

You remind Dr. Fied that this search committee will not be your first such assignment. Four years ago, you chaired the committee that led to the hiring of the current provost, devoting a great deal of time and energy to that effort. "And do you remember what happened?" you ask Dr. Fied. "After a year and a half of work, we recommended a candidate to the president. She thanked us for our recommendation and then hired someone who wasn't even on our short list. It was a purely political appointment. She never even had the courtesy to explain her decision to the committee. I'm still dealing with colleagues who think that those of us who served on the search committee actually *did* recommend the president's choice. And we all know what a disaster *that's* been. So, I'm not going to waste my time and put my courses and research on a back burner again after an experience like that. If you want me on the search committee, you're simply going to have to lighten my load."

Dr. Fied becomes angry. "This is what drives me crazy about this university," Dr. Fied says. "Faculty members keep telling us that they want a greater role in shared governance, but every time we offer them one, they try to leverage it simply for their own benefit. If you really cared about the university instead of just yourself, you'd understand how important this search committee is. Look: Either do it or don't do it, but don't use a pretense of participating in shared governance as a way of holding me hostage for a reduced teaching load."

"Well, I think you've answered all my questions," you reply coolly. "Have a nice day and good luck finding anyone to serve on your search committee." You get up and leave Dr. Fied's office.

1. Was your response both justified and appropriate?

2. Is this issue genuinely one of shared governance as Dr. Fied alleges?

3. How did your past experience on the previous search committee complicate this situation?

4. Certainly, the president is authorized to select the provost, and even you noted that your committee merely "*recommended* a candidate." What might the president have done in the past to avoid the conflict you just had with the associate dean?

5. Are there policies that could have been in place so that this problem could have been avoided?

6. What are the relevant higher education principles of inclusion by various groups in decision making that affect this scenario?

7. How could better communication and collegiality have altered the outcome of this scenario?

8. Does this scenario suggest that there are problems at your institution arising from a lack of trust between the administration and faculty, or is some other issue involved?

9. If you actually were the person involved in this scenario, would it have occurred to you that there might be negative repercussions (perhaps affecting promotion, merit increases, or teaching assignments) resulting from your refusal to serve on the search committee? Would those possible repercussions have affected your decision?

10. To what extent does Dr. Fied "cause" this conflict? To what extent do *you* cause it?

Case Study # 3: Changing the Rules … in the Middle of the Game

You are a tenured full professor in a department that has a well-earned reputation as one of your institution's best. It is highly respected by students, administrators, and other faculty members and is led by a chair, Dr. Stella Reputation, whom almost everyone on campus regards as a preeminent scholar and academic leader. To the best of your recollection, there has never been even a single instance of incivility among the faculty in your program. You and your colleagues enjoy coming to work and thrive in the environment that Dr. Reputation has created.

This year your service assignment includes heading the Department Evaluation Task Force (DETF), a committee of three members that is responsible for reviewing each full-time faculty member's credentials and making recommendations to the chair regarding reappointment, tenure, promotion in rank, and merit pay. The committee's recommendations have always been supported by Dr. Reputation, probably because decisions by this group have routinely been unanimous and because the members of the committee are all considered "opinion leaders" by their peers. As the task force begins its review, you discover that one of your departmental colleagues, Dr. Nada Researcher, has applied for tenure and the rank of associate professor. In annual evaluations, your university uses a three-level ranking system: *Does Not Meet Expectations*, *Meets Expectations*, and *Exceeds Expectations*. For five straight years, the DETF has given Dr. Researcher a rating of *Exceeds Expectations* and Dr. Reputation always concurred with this recommendation.

But although Dr. Researcher has performed exceptional service to the department, college and institution (serving as the department's representative to the university-wide curriculum committee, generally recognized as a major service role) and is an outstanding teacher (with the highest student and peer evaluations in the program), her level of scholarship hasn't matched her achievements in these other areas. She has published only a single article in a relatively obscure journal and hasn't submitted any proposals for external grants. This area of weakness was, of course, noted in her annual evaluations, but her work in other areas was so impressive that it was believed to compensate for an area where you fully expected her to improve in the future.

Two years ago, a new president came to the university, Dr. Ree Searchwun, the former provost of Highly Endowed University. The cornerstone of Dr. Searchwun's strategic plan is elevating your university to the status of having Very High Research Activity, according to the Carnegie classification system for doctoral-granting institutions. One of her first appointments was a new provost, Dr. Isla Blige, who was charged with the task of making your school "a world-class research university" as quickly as possible. Dr. Searchwun and Dr. Blige are almost relentless in their single-minded pursuit of "research excellence." Funding has been diverted from pedagogical areas to start-up funding for incoming scholars, and the only topics the president and provost ever seem to talk about are research, the football team, and the need for everyone to "get with the program."

The Faculty Senate has tried to work with the president and provost to achieve their goals while becoming a bit more flexible in their approach, citing your school's long-standing reputation as a teaching institution, but to no avail. Teaching loads have increased. Advising loads have mushroomed. A new Division of Research has been created, further draining funds from instructional support. And the plans to build your department's long-promised classroom building have been scrapped in favor of constructing additional laboratory space for other disciplines and a lavish new home for the Division of Research. It is not a complete shock, therefore, when Dr. Researcher's application for promotion and tenure, after having received the unanimous support of both the college and university review committees, was vetoed by the provost. Dr. Researcher appealed this decision to the president who upheld the decision of Dr. Blige. Dr. Researcher was thus placed on a terminal contract and will have to leave the university at the end of next year.

1. If you *had* to choose one of the following responses, which would you choose? Why?

    a. I would ask the chair to call a departmental meeting to discuss Dr. Researcher's case and decide on an appropriate response.

    b. I would file a grievance against the provost on Dr. Researcher's behalf.

    c. I would file a grievance against the president on Dr. Researcher's behalf.

    d. I would appeal the decision of the president and provost to the governing board on Dr. Researcher's behalf.

    e. I would resign as a member of the Department Evaluation Task Force.

    f. I would do everything in my power to help Dr. Researcher find another job.

    g. I would meet with the other members of the DETF and develop a united plan of action.

    h. I would work with the Faculty Senate to develop a united plan of action.

    i. I would contact the American Association of University Professors to learn about viable options.

    j. I would contact news outlets about this issue.

    k. I would ask Dr. Researcher what *she* wanted me to do.

2. If your options were *not* limited to those listed under #1, what would you do?

Case Study #4: A Tale of Two Presidents

You're a tenured full professor who has been elected to serve as the president of the Faculty Senate. Recently your university has also hired a new CEO, and you're looking forward to working with her in a cooperative manner. Although you haven't previously met the new president, she has a reputation for being a strong-willed no-nonsense sort of person who follows through on decisions once she makes them. She was a controversial choice in the eyes of the faculty, but the school's governing board supported her hiring unanimously.

The reason why the faculty wasn't comfortable with having this particular candidate named president relates to some information that came out during the search committee's reference calls. The faculty of the university where she last served had indicated that she was consistently "pro-administration" and thus, in your mind as well as in the minds of many of your colleagues, "anti-faculty." Her style during the interview process was also rather abrupt, and she seemed to give more time to questions posed by board members and the vice presidents than to those of the faculty.

Even so, you're an optimist by nature, and you've decided that you're willing to give a chance to anyone who has just entered a tough new position. In your capacity as president of the Faculty Senate, therefore, you arrange a special reception on the new president's first day on the job so that members of the faculty can meet her informally and welcome her to the institution. Although the reception begins at 2:30, it's nearly 3:15 before the new president arrives. She makes no apology for being late and, after only a minute or two of meeting each attendee, she pats them on the shoulder and moves on to the next person. After about half an hour, she taps a spoon on a glass to attract everyone's attention.

"Excuse me, everyone, but I think it would just be easier if I spoke to everyone at once rather that repeating myself over and over. I think you all know that your school has faced a number of challenges recently. Budgets have been tight, hiring has been frozen, and enrollment has dipped. I think there are two reasons for this. First, you haven't been making adequate use of the resources you have. I was walking through the halls earlier today, and I noticed that three or four classrooms were empty (even in the middle of the day!) and that at least half a dozen faculty members didn't seem to be in their offices. Second, you haven't recognized the changing nature of today's student body. Students want classes to be offered whenever they want them, not at a time that best suits your own personal schedules."

She goes on to note that, because of her vision and mandate for change, your school will now become your area's first "24/7 University." Some classes might begin at 2:00 am or later. "You students are awake then. Why aren't you?" she asks. "You need to offer classes whenever your customers want them." Saturday will be a class day, you're informed, as will Sunday. "I shouldn't have to remind you of this, but apparently I do: The students are our customers, and you haven't been serving our customers very well. That is about to change."

You feel foolish for your earlier optimism and think it's ironic that you were planning to tell the new president what a great faculty the school has and what a wonderful place it is to work. As you look around the room, you see that everyone else seems to be as stunned as you are. Maybe this wasn't the best year to head the Faculty Senate after all.

1. If you *had* to choose one of the following responses, which would you choose? Why?

    a. I would resign from my position as president of the Faculty Senate.

    b. I would use my position as president of the Faculty Senate to call for a vote of no confidence in the new president.

    c. I would contact members of the governing board to protest the way the faculty is being treated by the new president.

    d. I would contact the alumni association to explain the problems resulting from the hiring of a president who doesn't seem to understand the basic concepts of shared governance.

    e. I would contact the American Association of University Professors and encourage them to become actively involved in the challenges the faculty is facing under the new president.

    f. I would contact the legislature and use the media to draw attention to the challenges the faculty is facing under the new president.

2. If your options were *not* limited to those listed under #1, what would you do?

Case Study #5: The Problem of Choice

A generous donor has made a gift of $25 million to your university, stipulating that this money can only be used for one of the two following projects:

1. Educational infrastructure in the form of building high technology classrooms, or

2. Capital improvements that enhance student life, such as a new food court or a fitness center.

"I don't want my gift to be watered down by doing either of these things halfway," the donor told the Advancement Office. "So, don't try to split the gift between the two projects. And don't use it for anything other than one of the two purposes I've outlined. If you try to do that, I'll rescind the gift and give it to Archrival Community College, understand?"

1. How should the school go about choosing which project to fund?

2. Which of the two options do you think the faculty would want?

3. Which of the two options do you think the upper administration would want?

4. Which of the two options do you think students would want?

5. Which of the two options do you think would benefit the greatest number of people at the university?

6. Which of the two options do you think would be most sustainable over time?

7. Which of the two options do you think would best raise the stature of the institution?

8. Who should be consulted about this choice?

9. Who should *make* this decision?

10. What role should the donor have in making this decision?

Case Study #6: Free Speech for Whom?

For years now, your institution has sponsored a "Book of the Year" program where all incoming students read the same book as a community-building exercise, and the author is invited to campus. This year's book was selected by the faculty because it had a theme of inclusion and the challenges faced by minority populations in society and in the justice system. You and other faculty members regarded this book as an innocuous choice.

It has turned out to be anything but innocuous.

You dismissed the first complaints as "students simply being students." A number of entering students complained about being "forced to read this book over the summer when we're not even technically enrolled yet and not receiving course credit for it." Some students even defaced the book and mailed it back.

The next wave of complaints were, however, much more serious. At a public presentation by the author, one student got up and shouted, "What right do you have to come here and shove your ideas down our throats? I pay good money to attend this school. I shouldn't have to endure indoctrination at your hands or from the faculty either." Other students then voiced their support for what the student had said and, despite several attempts to continue the presentation, the author was shouted down. The presentation ended in chaos.

Later that evening, protests against the book and its author were organized on campus. A group of more than a hundred students gathered outside the student union, stacked up the books from the "Book of the Year" program, and set them ablaze. For the next several days, local newspapers and television stations carried images of the book burning. a great deal of negative publicity about the institution appeared in the media. The story even attracted national attention.

You were not surprised that the president and provost called an emergency meeting of the faculty to deal with this issue. What you *were* surprised about, however, was the message you received from the upper administration. Rather than supporting the faculty, the president and provost held the faculty, not the students, at fault for the situation.

"I've been saying this for a long time," the president said. "This is exactly what happens when we sacrifice education for indoctrination." You wince when you observe that the president has repeated the vocabulary used by the angry student on the night of the protest. "There's altogether too much political correctness on this campus. You've got to shut this down."

Uncertain about exactly what the president means by "this," you nonetheless ask, "But what about academic freedom and freedom of speech?"

"I'm very glad you brought up freedom of speech," the president replies, "because that's exactly what the students are doing: They're exercising their right of free speech by shouting down speakers they find offensive and burning books that contain hateful ideas. And as for academic freedom ... I'm glad you brought that up, too. Yesterday, at an emergency session of the governing board, we decided to exert *our* academic freedom. From now on, *we'll* decide on what book incoming students will read."

"Who's 'we'?" you ask.

"Haven't you been listening?" the president responds with a disdainful look. "The administration and the governing board. Not the faculty. You've lost your right to choose the book that'll be used because you tried to subvert what should have been an educational activity to a political one. *We're* back in charge now."

You find yourself thinking, "Can they do that?"

Questions

1. *Can* they in fact do that?

2. As a faculty member, what should be your response at this point?

3. What do you believe the faculty should do, moving forward?

Discussions of the Case Studies

As we said at the beginning of these case studies, be sure that you've decided what you would recommend before continuing to read our recommendations. The purpose of a case study isn't to give you the one "right" answer; it's to provide you with practice in thinking through complex situations before you have to deal with leadership challenges at your own institution. The cases we present aren't likely to occur in exactly the way we've written them during your own career, but thinking through these issues can help to refine your own leadership skills and decision-making methods. In addition, your own circumstances may mean that the best answer for you isn't necessarily the best answer for someone else. So, our recommendations are based on our own training and experience as academic leaders, but we can't be aware of all the conditions that might make our suggestions less than appropriate in your particular situation. With these disclaimers in mind, let's proceed to the case studies you've just encountered.

In **Case Study #1: Who's Responsible for Class Size?** We're presented with a situation in which both Dean Deane and your colleagues adopt rather extreme positions. Fortunately, for the vast number of us who work in higher education, neither our supervisors nor our colleagues are quite as unreasonable as the people in this scenario. But here's the point of this case study: From the perspective of many administrators (and for this case study you as chair may see yourself as an administrator), faculty responses to institutional requirements can sometimes *seem* as unreasonable as those outlined in this case. And from the perspective of many faculty members (and for this case study you as chair may also see yourself as a member of the faculty), administrative mandates can sometimes *seem* as unreasonable as those outlined imposed by Dean Deane.

From a shared governance perspective, both sides in this dispute actually have right on their side. The administration *can* set recruitment and retention targets, and the faculty *can* set academic requirements for majors (unless other policies of the institution specifically state that the program is not able to offer limited access to its courses or major). For this reason, even though your colleagues in this scenario have taken an extreme stance, their strategy is not entirely misguided. Remember what we said earlier about the role that veto power can play in a distributed organization. The faculty is essentially "vetoing" the dean's mandate. The result will thus probably be anger and threats, followed by some type of negotiation and "horse trading." Since the dean has the authority to authorize new hires, the faculty might propose that they'll take on additional responsibilities recruiting new students if she'll allocate two new faculty positions that can help alleviate the already unwieldy student-to-teacher ratio. In return, since the faculty has the authority to set curricular standards, the dean might propose that they drop their stringent new requirements and modify the curriculum to make it easier for students to graduate in a timely manner; in return, she might alleviate some of their workload by waiving certain service requirements and increasing their budget for student employees.

In addition, this scenario is clearly one that can benefit from improved communication. Channeling all demands and counter-demands through the department chair, as it is in the scenario, is unproductive. In a joint meeting with the full faculty, the dean could explain why higher recruitment and retention rates are necessary. Perhaps she is under pressure herself from the provost or president. Perhaps the institution is highly selective, and most departments do indeed have both very large enrollments and 98 percent retention rates. Perhaps other factors are behind her decision. In return, the faculty can better explain its pedagogy and the negative impact that increased recruitment and retention rates will have on student success. Perhaps the discipline's professional organization will not accredit programs that go beyond a certain student-to-teacher ratio. Perhaps safety concerns or the capacity of laboratories and classrooms limit course sections to a certain size. Perhaps expectations from employers and graduate programs require students to have close faculty supervision. Each side in this discussion has certain rights according to generally accepted principles of shared governance and may well have reasons for taking the position that it has, but those matters will never be communicated unless there is a candid discussion between the administration and faculty.

Case Study # 2: Different Perspectives on Shared Governance brings us face-to-face with one of the challenges of working at a university today: Faculty members do indeed want a major role in making institutional decisions, but doing so requires a major time commitment that they often don't have because of their teaching, research, and service responsibilities. In addition, the changing nature of the modern university (not to mention the fact that limited budgets seem to become more limited every year) means that faculty members are routinely asked to do more and more—help recruit students, engage in fundraising, write grant proposals, perform outcomes assessment and program reviews—even as enrollment caps in courses are raised and staff positions are eliminated.

This case study also involves another challenge that can sometimes result when we're dealing with shared governance: Administrators sometimes merely go through the motions of "consulting" the faculty even though they've already decided what they're going to do. Such a practice severely undermines the faculty's faith in the effectiveness of shared governance. Make no mistake about it: The president in this scenario was perfectly entitled to choose whoever she wanted as provost. But after such a time-consuming process (eighteen months of work!), selecting a candidate who wasn't even on the search committee's short list *gives the impression* that the president didn't value the faculty members' contributions. A common faculty assumption is that upper administrators simply "consult" the faculty because they think it makes them *look* inclusive, but that they are going to do what they want anyway. That appears to be the impression you received in this scenario, and it serves as an impediment to your ability to trust the administration when asked for your "advice."

Both of these factors have complicated the ability for you and Dr. Fied to have a constructive conversation about the dean's search. The associate dean is frustrated by the faculty's desire to be active in shared governance while simultaneously refusing opportunities to do so. As we mentioned earlier in this guide, that's a common sentiment among college administrators today. Similarly, your sense that your earlier advice was ignored has left you feeling "once burned, twice shy." Perhaps for that reason neither you nor Dr. Fied in this scenario are communicating in the most collegial manner. If even one of you had taken a slightly different approach, the conversation may have had a different outcome. What this case study suggests, therefore, is that a (re)building of trust is often a prerequisite to meaningful shared governance at many colleges and universities. If the faculty and administration don't trust one another, they're not going to be open to the idea that the recommendations others make are intended to benefit the institution, not merely themselves.

For **Case Study # 3: Changing the Rules ... in the Middle of the Game**, let's imagine that the scenario continues as follows. The department chair, Dr. Reputation, arranges for herself and the members of the Department Evaluation Task Force to meet jointly with both the president and the provost to discuss Dr. Researcher's case. In this meeting, you're asked to speak on behalf of the faculty in the department. You acknowledge the fact that it is clearly the president's responsibility to either accept or reject the recommendations of all parties in this case. But you also note that Dr. Researcher is an extremely valuable member of the department. You cite her many accomplishments in teaching, service, and advising. You refer to the fact that she received a rating of *Exceed Expectations* each year since her hiring. And you note that, even though universities are entitled to change evaluation criteria, Dr. Researcher wasn't given sufficient time to meet these new criteria, which hadn't even been outlined at the time of her hiring. You note that Dr. Researcher might have grounds to sue the university for wrongful dismissal, and you go on to cite several recent cases where this has occurred.

"Until tenure has been granted, Dr. Researcher is a probationary employee," Dr. Searchwun replies. "She can be non-renewed for any reason or for *no* reason. So, let her sue. She wouldn't win."

"Maybe not," you agree. "But the time we'd all spend—yourself included—giving depositions and going to trial is time that we wouldn't be spending making our school a Research 1 university. Besides, with all the trouble the football team has been having this year, it doesn't seem like a good time for more negative publicity in the newspaper and the local media. I can think of several dozen faculty members off the top of my head who have rather strong feelings about this issue and who would inevitably want to speak out. The school's going to receive a very black eye in the Court of Public Opinion," you conclude, unnecessarily mixing your metaphors.

"We won't give in to threats!" the provost shouts.

"Why, Dr. Blige," you reply with an air of feigned innocence and surprise, "I'm not saying any of this as a threat. I'm actually just trying to advance the president's strategic goals and protect the reputation of the university. Shouldn't we all just 'get with the program'?"

After some additional discussion, the president and provost suggest that perhaps a compromise could be made: Suppose Dr. Researcher's tenure clock were extended for three more years with the understanding that she would meet specific research goals that Dr. Reputation, Dr. Blige, and the dean would all agree on jointly.

"What about any other faculty members turned down for promotion or tenure on the basis of insufficient research this year?" you ask. "It would seem equitable to ..."

"We'll offer the same opportunity to them," Dr. Blige responds, her teeth somewhat clenched.

"Excellent then," Dr. Reputation concludes. "You see what we can accomplish if we all take shared governance seriously?"

Does the way in which we've just concluded this scenario fall into the domain of pure fantasy? Probably. But it does illustrate a key point. Shared governance succeeds best when each segment of the university—notably the governing board, administration, and faculty—recognize that their powers are limited and that they can only achieve their goals if they provide something one of the other segments *wants* in return for something that they themselves *need*. In our (admittedly idealized) conclusion of this scenario, you focused on the desire of the upper administration to increase the school's research profile and avoid bad publicity. You also acknowledged their interest in the success of the football team as a way of applying a little more leverage. You couldn't *compel* the president and provost to be more flexible but, based on the areas that you as a faculty member do control, you created an environment in which they *wanted* to be more flexible. Even if the scenario was indeed somewhat fantastic, that's actually how certain aspects of shared governance work "in the real world." We provide incentives for others to make a few concessions.

Your initial response to **Case Study #4: A Tale of Two Presidents** might be "Well, here is more fantasy again. If the ending of the last scenario was a utopian fantasy, then this case study is simply dystopian. No new president can ever be *that* bad." Au contraire, dear reader; Bob and Jeff are both here to tell you that they've met and (who's telling?) maybe even *served* under new presidents that were even worse than the one described in this case study. So, if you think we're making this stuff up, maybe you've just been lucky so far in the administrators you've met.

But before you conclude that you'd go charging into this situation with guns blazing, pause a moment. Unless you're also a woman who has risen to a senior administrative position, you may not be aware of all the challenges this new president had to overcome just to reach her current level. She may have had to prove that she was tougher, more decisive, and less likely to be taken advantage of than any ten men who wanted her job. She may also have other pressures placed on her that you don't learn about from this scenario. Extending the class schedule may have been a requirement of her hiring imposed on her by the governing board. She may have been told that she had one year to solve problems you aren't even aware of and may not have time for some of the "niceties" of attending the meet-and-greet that you were expecting. Besides, did you consider your own role in what just happened? Was it a good idea to schedule this reception on the new president's *very first day*? She may have a lot of work that she needs to get done, work that your inconvenient scheduling just made harder, and her exasperation may be, in part at least, your fault.

In addition, look beyond the president's brusque style. Many traditional-aged college students *are* up late at night. Some *may* want more weekend classes, particularly if they're juggling jobs, family obligations, and school during the regular workweek. So, while the president's mandate may initially seem ridiculous, there are aspects of it that may actually have some merit. In fact, if it were one of your colleagues who proposed this idea in the Faculty Senate, would you be willing to dismiss it out of hand?

And therein lies the crux of this case study. The new president has created a problem because of her *style*, not necessarily because of the *substance* of what she's demanding. As a new president, she may not even be aware of procedures in place that make it impossible for her simply to extend the course schedule by fiat. So, ask yourself the following question: As the new president of the Faculty Senate, suppose that you had alienated the administration by insisting on a change that wasn't even within your purview to change? Suppose your style had come across as inflexible and abrupt when you saw yourself as merely being decisive and persistent? How would *you* want to be treated in such a case?

Then go and do likewise with regard to your institution's new president.

Case Study #5: The Problem of Choice presents us with the *good* type of problem: In this scenario, we're faced with unforeseen riches to spend and now only have to decide how best to spend them. If you're a faculty member, we have some bad news. While you may well be consulted about this decision, it's highly unlikely that you're going to be allowed to *make* the decision. But if you're an administrator, we have some bad news, too: Whatever decision you make, you're still going to have a lot of people mad at you.

Probably the best approach the institution can take to decide its approach is to hold open meetings where all constituencies can offer their advice. Make it clear from the beginning who or which group will make the final decision but give everyone a chance to be heard. Decide early on the principles that will be used when the decision is made. Will the funding be used to advance a goal of the strategic plan? If so, then what priority is given to high technology classrooms in the strategic plan? What priority is given to new student service facilities? Or will the funding be used *outside* of the strategic plan? That may initially seem to be a counterintuitive suggestion but remember that this gift was unexpected. It gives the institution a chance to do something above and beyond what it was going to do anyway. This gift could be transformative, in other words, not merely operational.

Recognize, too, that the criteria used to make the decision may privilege one choice over another. In the questions following the case study, you were asked, "Which of the two options do you think would benefit the greatest number of people at the university?" If most of your students don't take advantage of facilities like a food court or fitness room, choosing that criterion might give the edge to selecting the new classroom building for the project. On the other hand, you were also asked, "Which of the two options do you think would be most sustainable over time?" If the food court or fitness room were revenue-raising enterprises while the classroom building was so high tech that it would have to be upgraded frequently, choosing that criterion might give the edge to selecting the student service facility for the project.

The most important conclusion to draw from this case study, therefore, is that the situation presented here is really a matter of shared *consultation*, not really shared *governance*. Members of the faculty, staff, and student body often don't see the difference between those two concepts. That's why conversations about what shared governance is—and even more importantly, what it *isn't*—need to be frequent and ongoing.

Case Study #6: Free Speech for Whom? confronts us with the gravest of gray areas. If the question involved a textbook used in a course with an approved syllabus, the answer to the question "Can they do that?" would be *no*. The established principles of academic freedom and shared governance delegate curricular matters—including what is taught and how it is taught—to the faculty. But what is the "Book of the Year" program at this institution? Is it an extracurricular activity, like an athletic event? If so, the administration and governing board may well have the right to make the decision they did? Is it a curricular activity, like a first-year seminar? Then no, the faculty members would have the right to choose the book. Is it a co-curricular activity, like a French club? *That's* where the gray area comes in because co-curricular activities support the curriculum but, since they are not credit-producing, are not technically *in* the curriculum. In that case, the history of the "Book of the Year" program might provide some guidance. Who initiated this program, the faculty or others at the institution? Who serves on the oversight committee for the program? In which budget is the program funded?

One might hope that, in the real world, a president of an institution wouldn't oppose the faculty in this way. After all, in the United States, shouting down a speaker is, despite the president's claims, not protected speech under the First Amendment. Shouting down a speaker entails unlawful disruption of regular business and authorized campus activities. (See Gillman and Chemerinsky, 2017.) And burning books sets a bad precedent, not to mention invoking unpleasant historical parallels. It would be unfortunate, indeed, for a president to be seen as supporting such activities.

Unfortunate, perhaps, but not unknown. There are instances of administrators and governing boards who view the faculty, not as a co-equal partner at a college or university, but as "the enemy." Or if calling the faculty "the enemy" is too strong, there are administrators and governing boards who regard faculty members as out of touch with "the real world" and as little more than employees who should follow instructions rather than speak their minds.

What should you do if you're a faculty member who finds yourself in a situation like this? Do your homework. Find out exactly what responsibilities are delegated to the governing board, administration, and faculty at your school and in which domain the activity you're concerned about falls. Consult an attorney with expertise in higher education law. Consult your union or professional organization. While your rights are not unlimited, neither are those of any other partner in shared governance. If you don't defend your rights, you become complicit in their elimination.

CHAPTER 11

A Role Play About Shared Governance

One additional tool that colleges and universities can use to promote understanding of shared governance is a role play. In this type of exercise, the participants play the parts of different stakeholder groups at the institution. They then try to adopt the perspective of that constituency, ask the sort of questions someone from that group might ask, and adopt the sort of perspective members of that group are likely to share.

The best role plays are those in which the participants assume the identity of a group different from their own. Students would then try to see the world as faculty members see it. Faculty members try to see the world through the perspective of the governing board. Of course, that's not always possible. If you conduct this exercise at a faculty retreat, for instance, only faculty members may be participating. The point is, however, that if you have a mixed group of participants, the exercise works better when people are forced to approach issues differently from how they usually do.

The core exercise would be conducted by dividing participants into at least the three core groups of the distributed model or organizations for higher education that was depicted in Figure 3 above:

- Members of the governing board
- Members of the upper administration
- Members of the faculty

The exercise works the best if you have at least three people in each group. If you are conducting the exercise with twelve or more people, you might also want to consider adding additional constituent groups, such as:

- Students
- Middle management (deans, directors, department chairs, and so on)
- Legislators

   ○ Major donors

   ○ Alumni

The precise number and identity of these additional stakeholder groups really depends only on the size of the exercise and the most important (or perhaps most vocal) stakeholder groups at your institution.

Once you've assigned your groups, your next task is to imagine that, for whatever reason, all of these groups are present at the same meeting where one or more decisions have to be made. Each group is instructed to present the perspective that it believes would be taken by the constituency it represents. The "meeting" then proceeds to see whether a decision about the issue can be made.

You can organize the discussion however you like. If you assign each group a time limit and insist that other groups must remain silent while one group is speaking, you'll have a more orderly activity. If you let everyone speak whenever he or she likes, your "meeting" may break down in chaos. That chaos may be quite valuable, however: It illustrates for the participants precisely what can happen in shared governance if allowance isn't made for others to present their points of view. For that reason, you may wish to start with a disorderly, open discussion and, when progress proves to be impossible, draw a conclusion about the need for each constituency to listen to the others in a collegial and constructive manner. At that point, you could proceed with a time limit assigned to each group.

The activity can include one agenda item or several, depending on the amount of time you have available. This role play works best, however, when a number of items are up for discussion. As participants will learn throughout the exercise, different constituencies tend to take ownership of different kinds of decisions. That, indeed, is a central aspect of shared governance.

You may choose one or more of the following items for your agenda in this role play:

   ○ A proposal from the governing board to reduce staffing in disciplines related to the fine and performing arts and in the humanities in order to increase staffing and raise salaries in the STEM disciplines and professional programs.

   ○ A proposal from the upper administration to reduce costs by converting at least 90% of instruction to an online format (retaining in-person instruction only for the most essential labs and practica) and to offer as many courses as possible in an asynchronous (24/7/365) format.

- A proposal from the faculty to replace "seat time" with "competency standards" as a basis for earning credit in all courses.

- A proposal from the governing board to replace tenure (or the possibility of long-term contracts) with annual contracts.

- A proposal from the upper administration that all decisions related to curriculum, hiring, promotion, and contract renewal be submitted to the governing board as part of an "informational agenda" rather than a "consent agenda."

- A proposal from the faculty to expand the promotion system to include three new ranks about the rank of full professor: distinguished professor, eminent professor, and illustrious professor. Faculty members will also be able to decide, once in each rank, whether they would pursue a teaching track or a research track.

- A proposal from students that a weeklong pre-final-exam study period (i.e., an extended "reading day") be scheduled before each final exam period, requiring an extension of the school year.

- A proposal from the athletics director that special sections be created for any courses taken by varsity athletes, with these sections built around the athletic schedule rather than the academic calendar to improve the ability of athletes to keep up with their coursework.

The most important part of this activity occurs after the role play has ended. What have the participants learned about the perspectives of different constituent groups? Which approaches to decision making are more effective than others in the context of shared governance? How has the activity shaped the participants' own views about shared governance?

An instruction sheet that may be given to the participants appears on the following two pages. Photocopy these sheets, assign each participant to one group, and choose which proposal(s) the imaginary meeting will address.

SHARED GOVERNANCE ROLE PLAY

DIRECTIONS: In this role play, we will imagine that a meeting is taking place among various constituent groups. You will be assigned to one of these constituent groups. For the remainder of the role play, try to adopt the perspective of the group to which you've been assigned. What position would that group take on the issue(s) under discussion? How would they present and defend that position? How might they try to persuade other constituencies that their position is correct?

The constituent group to which you are assigned is the _____.

The purpose of the meeting is to decide whether one or more of the following proposals is adopted. Assume, for the purpose of this exercise, that <u>each constituent group gets one vote</u> regarding each proposal.

The meeting today will decide on the following proposal(s):

- [ ] A proposal from the governing board to reduce staffing in disciplines related to the fine and performing arts and in the humanities in order to increase staffing and raise salaries in the STEM disciplines and professional programs.

- [ ] A proposal from the upper administration to reduce costs by converting at least 90% of instruction to an online format (retaining in-person instruction only for the most essential labs and practica) and to offer as many courses as possible in an asynchronous (24/7/365) format.

- [ ] A proposal from the faculty to replace "seat time" with "competency standards" as a basis for earning credit in all courses.

- [ ] A proposal from the governing board to replace tenure (or the possibility of long-term contracts) with annual contracts.

- [ ] A proposal from the upper administration that all decisions related to curriculum, hiring, promotion, and contract renewal be submitted to the governing board as part of an "informational agenda" rather than a "consent agenda."

- [ ] A proposal from the faculty to expand the promotion system to include three new ranks about the rank of full professor: distinguished professor, eminent professor, and illustrious professor. Faculty members will also be able to decide, once in each rank, whether they would pursue a teaching track or a research track.

- [ ] A proposal from students that a weeklong pre-final-exam study period (i.e., an extended "reading day") be scheduled before each final exam period, requiring an extension of the school year.

(Keep reading; more instructions follow.)

☐ A proposal from the athletics director that special sections be created for any courses taken by varsity athletes, with these sections built around the athletic schedule rather than the academic calendar to improve the ability of athletes to keep up with their coursework.

In this exercise, the constituency group(s) that my group had the most difficult time working with was/were:

The issues that most concerned my constituency group were:

The negotiation or leadership strategy that proved *most* effective for my group was:

The negotiation or leadership strategy that proved *least* effective for my group was:

References

Administrator Evaluations Task Force. (2013). *Guidelines and procedures for the TWU Administrator Evaluation Process (AEP) by faculty.* https://twu.edu/media/documents/faculty-senate/July_2013_Guidelines_for_Faculty_Senate_Administrator_Eva.pdf.

Association of Governing Boards. (2010). *Association of Governing Boards of Universities and Colleges statement on board responsibility for institutional governance.* Washington, DC: Association of Governing Boards. https://agb.org/wp-content/uploads/2019/01/statement_2010_institutional_governance.pdf.

Birnbaum, R. (2004). The end of shared governance: Looking ahead of looking back? In W.G. Tierney and V. Lechuga (eds.), *Restructuring shared governance in higher education. New Directions in Higher Education.* 127, 5-22. San Francisco, CA: Jossey-Bass.

Campus Governance Leaders Toolkit: State University of New York. (2019). https://www.suny.edu/about/shared-governance/sunyvoices/cgl-toolkit/shared-governance/.

Cipriano, R. E., & Riccardi, R. (2009). The state of shared governance. *AAUP Vanguard. 29*(2), 4-5.

Del Favero, M. (2003). Faculty-administrator relationships as integral to high-performing governance systems: New frameworks for study. *American Behavioral Scientist. 46,* 902-922.

Fish, S. (2007). Shared governance: Democracy is not an educational ideal. *Change. 39*(2), 9-13.

Gillman, C., & Chemerinsky, H. (2017). Does disruption violate free speech? *The Chronicle of Higher Education.* https://www.chronicle.com/article/Does-Disruption-Violate-Free/241470.

Hutchins, R. M. (1936). *Higher learning in America.* New Haven, CT: Yale University Press.

Kezar, A., Lester, J., & Anderson, G. (2006). Challenging stereotypes that interfere with effective governance. *Thought and Action.* Washington, D.C.: National Education Association. 121-134.

Olson, G. (2009). Exactly what is 'Shared Governance'? *The Chronicle of Higher Education.* https://www.chronicle.com/article/exactly-what-is-shared-governance/?

cid2=gen_login_refresh&cid=gen_sign_in&cid2=gen_login_refresh.

Principles and Practices of Shared Governance: The University of Louisiana at Monroe. (2007). https://www.ulm.edu/sharedgovernance/documents/ulm_principles_of_shared_governance.pdf.

Rhoades, G. (2005). Capitalism, academic style, and shared governance. *Academe*. 91(3), 38-42. http://www.nea.org/assets/img/PubThoughtAndAction/TAA_06_12.pdf.

Shared Governance: The University of Baltimore. (2019). http://www.ubalt.edu/about-ub/shared-governance/.

Shared Governance: The University of Louisiana at Monroe. (2019). https://www.ulm.edu/sharedgovernance/.

Shared Governance at the UW. (2019). https://www.washington.edu/informed-choice/shared-governance/.

Simmons, D. L. (2009). Shared governance in the University of California: An overview. https://senate.universityofcalifornia.edu/_files/resources/SHRDGOV-09Revision.pdf.

Statement on Government of Colleges and Universities: America Association of University Professors. (n.d.) https://www.aaup.org/report/statement-government-colleges-and-universities.

Tierney, W. G., & Minor, J. T. (2003). *Challenges for governance: A national report*. Los Angeles, CA: Center for Higher Education Policy Analysis. https://files.eric.ed.gov/fulltext/ED482060.pdf.

Tierney, W. G. (2004). *Competing conceptions of academic governance: Negotiating the perfect storm*. Baltimore, MD: Johns Hopkins University Press.

Zaloom, C. (2019). The cost of college for the middle class. *The New York Times: Sunday Review*. September 1, 2019. 4.

Resources

Cramer, S. F. (2017). *Shared governance in higher education: Volume 1, Demands, transitions, transformations.* Albany, NY: State University of New York Press.

Cramer, S. F. (2017). *Shared governance in higher education: Volume 2, New paradigms, evolving perspectives.* Albany, NY: State University of New York Press.

Guanci, G., & Medeiros, M. (2018). *Shared governance that works.* Minneapolis, MN: Creative Healthcare Management.

Porter-O'Grady, T. (1992). *Shared governance implementation manual.* St. Louis, MO: Mosby Year Book.

Tierney, W. G., & Lechuga, V. M. (2004). *Restructuring shared governance in higher education.* San Francisco, CA: Jossey-Bass

About the Authors

Robert E. Cipriano and Jeffrey L Buller are senior partners in ATLAS: Academic Training, Leadership, & Assessment Services.

Bob is former chair and professor emeritus of the department of Recreation and Leisure Studies at Southern Connecticut State University. He has a doctorate in Therapeutic Recreation, with an Area of Concentration in College Teaching. He is the author of five books, one on collegiality in higher education, one on the Special Olympics, and three books on academic leadership in higher education. He has written chapters in three additional textbooks, and has published more than 180 journal articles and manuscripts. He has been awarded more than $9 million in grants and contracts and delivered in excess of 260 presentations in the United States, Asia, and the Middle East.

Jeff holds a doctorate in classics from the University of Wisconsin-Madison. He is the author of over twenty books on academic leadership, a monograph on Wagnerian opera, a textbook for first-year college students, several novels, and more than 200 articles, essays, and reviews. In addition to conducting leadership-training workshops all over the world, he serves as a consultant to the Ministry of Higher Education in Saudi Arabia in its development of a region-wide Academic Leadership Center.

Books By ATLAS Authors

By Jeffrey L. Buller and Robert E. Cipriano

- *A Toolkit for College Professors*
- *A Toolkit for Department Chairs*

By Robert E. Cipriano

- *Facilitating a Collegial Department in Higher Education: Strategies for Success*

By Jeffrey L. Buller

- *Evaluating Boards and Administrators: Promoting Greater Accountability in Higher Education*
- *Confronting Today's Issues: Opportunities and Challenges for School Administrators* (with Chad Prosser and Denise Spirou)
- *A Handbook for College and University Advisory Boards* (with Dianne M. Reeves)
- *Mindful Leadership: An Insight-Based Approach to College Administration*
- *Managing Time and Stress: A Guide for Academic Leaders to Accomplish What Matters*
- *The Five Cultures of Academic Development: Crossing Boundaries in Higher Education Fundraising* (with Dianne M. Reeves)
- *Authentic Academic Leadership: A Values-Based Approach to College Administration*
- *Hire the Right Faculty Member Every Time*
- *Best Practices for Faculty Search Committees: How to Review Applications and Interview Candidates*
- *World-Class Fundraising Isn't a Solo Sport: The Team Approach to Academic Fundraising* (with Dianne M. Reeves)
- *Going for the Gold: How to Become a World-Class Academic Fundraiser* (with Dianne M. Reeves)
- *The Essential Academic Dean or Provost: A Comprehensive Desk Reference*, Second Edition

- *Building Leadership Capacity: A Guide to Best Practices* (with Walter H. Gmelch)
- *Change Leadership in Higher Education: A Practical Guide to Academic Transformation*
- *Positive Academic Leadership: How to Stop Putting Out Fires and Start Making a Difference*
- *Best Practices in Faculty Evaluation: A Practical Guide for Academic Leaders*
- *The Essential Department Chair: A Comprehensive Desk Reference, Second Edition*
- *Academic Leadership Day By Day: Small Steps That Lead to Great Success*
- *The Essential College Professor: A Practical Guide to an Academic Career*

ATLAS Guides

ATLAS Guides provide concise, field-tested advice that academic leaders can use for their own development or in leadership training programs. Each guide includes material from one of ATLAS' popular workshops, plus exercises, inventories, case studies, and resources for further study.

- *The ATLAS Guide to Leadership in Higher Education*
- *The ATLAS Guide to Promoting Collegiality in Higher Education*
- *The ATLAS Guide to Effective Meetings in Higher Education*
- *The ATLAS Guide to Effective Communication in Higher Education*
- *The ATLAS Guide to Emotional Intelligence in Higher Education*
- *The ATLAS Guide to Managing Conflict in Higher Education*
- *The ATLAS Guide to Career Development in Higher Education*
- *The ATLAS Guide to Coaching and Mentoring in Higher Education*
- *The ATLAS Guide to Shared Governance in Higher Education*
- *The ATLAS Guide to Leadership for Introverts in Higher Education*
- *The ATLAS Guide to Work/Life Balance in Higher Education*
- *The ATLAS Guide to Team Building in Higher Education*

About ATLAS

ATLAS: Academic Training, Leadership & Assessment Services offers training programs, books, and materials that deal with many aspects of academic leadership, fundraising, and board governance. Its programs include:

- Work-Life Balance
- Time Management
- Stress Management
- Conflict Management
- Promoting Teamwork
- Promoting Collegiality
- Communicating Effectively
- Introduction to Fundraising
- Leading Meetings Effectively
- Best Practices in Faculty Evaluation
- Decision Making and Problem Solving
- Change Leadership in Higher Education
- An Introduction to Academic Leadership
- Promoting Faculty and Staff Engagement
- Shared Governance: Only a Catchphrase?
- Best Practices in Coaching and Mentoring
- Career Development for College Professors
- The Introvert's Guide to Academic Leadership
- Best Practices in Faculty Recruitment and Hiring
- Protect Yourself from a Toxic Work Environment
- Freedom of Speech and Campus Civility: What Works?
- Moving Forward: Training and Development for Advisory Boards
- Motivation: How to Spur Yourself and Others on to Greater Things
- The Art of Small Talk: What Do I Say When I Fear I Have Nothing to Say?

- Developing Resilience as an Academic Leader: How to Bounce Back When Times Are Tough

- Authentic Academic Leadership: A Values-Based Approach to Academic Leadership

- Mindful Academic Leadership: An Insight-Based Approach to Academic Leadership

- Training the Trainers: How to Give Presentations and Provide Training the ATLAS Way

- Fostering a Collegial University: An In-Depth Exploration of Collegiality in Higher Education

- Managing Conflict: An In-Depth Exploration of Conflict Management in Higher Education

- Developing Leadership Capacity: How You Can Create a Leadership Development Program at Your Institution

- Why Academic Leaders Must Lead Differently: Understanding the Organizational Culture of Higher Education

- Getting Organized: Taking Control of Your Schedule, Workspace, and Habits to Get More Done in Less Time with Lower Stress

- Thriving in a Multi-Generational Work Environment: A Workshop for Academic Leaders

- Positive Academic Leadership: How to Stop Putting Out Fires and Start Making a Difference

For more information or to schedule one or more of these workshops at your college or university, contact:

ATLAS: Academic Training, Leadership & Assessment Services
9154 Wooden Road
Raleigh, NC 27617

800-355-6742

www.atlasleadership.com
questions@atlasleadership.com

Made in the USA
Monee, IL
21 January 2023

25812937R00044